MW01297848

Table of Contents:

Introduction

Do you feel like you are doing a lot of work without any real results? Are you distracted, overwhelmed with work pressure, and feeling disorganized? You are living a busy life, but are you living an organized and productive life?

We all want balance in work and life. We want to achieve that balance without being stressed out, overwhelmed and exhausted. The world is changing and you need to change and adjust with it.

An organized and productive person doesn't have more time in their day than you. We all live the same 24 hour day night cycle, but the difference between you and them is that they know how to manage their day properly.

This comprehensive book encourages you to take small steps in organizing your home, office, and life in order to enjoy a stress-free, productive life. Start your day after a quality sleep and with the proper diet and nutrition. You will remain active and organized all day.

Manage your stress and manage your day. In this book are simple techniques to help you learn how to become organized and get more things done in short time. Know about these productive methods and apply them in your life successfully.

These are useful tips for you to utilize every minute of your life, so don't waste time. Start reading the book and organize your life.

Chapter 1: Lifestyle Changes for an Organized and Productive Life

Lifestyle changes, such as improved sleeping, diet and exercise, can make a huge improvement in your life and make you organized and productive.

There is a correlation between the quality of sleep and a productive life.

An organized, productive life starts with a good night's sleep. Lack of sleep causes lowered levels of adrenaline and dopamine production in your body. Your body needs these hormones to regulate your attention and keep you focused on your work. This simply means that low levels of these hormones make you unproductive in your daily life. Quality sleep keeps you mentally sharp, emotionally balanced and full of energy and productive all day. Usually a healthy person needs 7 to 8 hours of quality sleep every night to perform efficiently during the day.

Tips for quality sleep:

- Set a fixed bedtime and wake-up time and strictly follow it, even on the weekends.

- Avoid naps during the day

- Prepare for sleep two hours before bedtime, and avoid any stimulating activity, such as family arguments, excess noise, violent TV shows or video games.

- Go to sleep only when you feel sleepy.

- While you are on the bed, don't watch the clock and turn it away from you.

- If you can't sleep even after 30 minutes, wake up and go to another room and do some quiet activity like reading. Only return to bed when you are feeling sleepy.

- Use your bed only for sleep and sex.

- Avoid caffeine after 12:00 noon.

- Avoid or limit smoking and alcohol during the day and totally avoid them 4 to 6 hours before bedtime.

- Don't eat a heavy meal just before bedtime.

- Make your bedroom sleep friendly. Lower lighting in the bedroom, adjust the temperature, and minimize noise.

Diet and nutrition for an organized life

You can only become your best when you consume a balanced, healthy diet. A balanced diet comprises of vitamins, minerals and other sources of nutrition. Most of the time your body converts the foods that you consume into glucose. Glucose is the fuel that runs your body and brain. Eat a wide variety of whole grains to have the most fruitful day possible.

Follow these eating tips for a productive day:

o Don't skip breakfast. Eat breakfast every morning and include complex carbohydrates, such as whole grain breads and cereals, in your breakfast.

o Eat frequent, small portion meals during the day. This eating habit will keep your glucose levels balanced and provide you a constant supply of energy to remain active all day. Avoid junk foods.

o You need fiber rich foods and plenty of water to remain active and productive all day. Eat fiber rich foods and drink at least 8 to 10 glasses of fluid a day.

o Drink a moderate amount of coffee only during the day. Consuming too much coffee is counterproductive to productivity. Limit or avoid alcohol before bedtime.

Eat foods that make you productive.

o *Dark leafy greens*: Dark leafy vegetables contain minerals, iron and phytonutrients. Iron increase blood flow to the brain cells and improves cognitive control of the brain, which is essential for a productive life.

o *Eggs*: Vitamin-B is the key for an active body, as it enhances memory and concentration and reduces the reaction time of your body. Organic eggs are rich with vitamin-B.

o *Salmon*: Salmon is rich with iron, Vitamin- B and omega-3. All are important for an active brain and body.

o *Berries*: Berries are rich with antioxidants, which improve your memory and keep you focused on the job.

o *Eggplant*: Eggplants improve communication between the brain cells and messenger molecules and keep your brain active and sharp.

o *Chocolate*: Dark chocolate increases your focus and concentration, and milk chocolate improves your verbal and visual memory.

o *Calcium rich foods*: Calcium rich foods are important for a productive mind and body. Foods such as low-fat milk, yogurt, and cheese are a good source of natural calcium.

o *Green tea*: Drinking green tea has a neuroprotective effect on the body and helps the nervous system work faster.

o *Garlic*: Garlic contains antiviral and antibacterial compounds and lowers stress related colds and infections.

Foods that are counterproductive to a productive day:

o Eating sugary foods make you weak, nervous and confused

o Junk food, such as hamburgers and French fries, slows your body's reaction time and make you sleepy when you work.

Eating too little is not helpful for a productive life.

Importance of exercise

Regular exercise improves your mental and physical health, increases your productivity and organizational skills. Benefits of exercise include:

- Regular exercise provides you energy and keeps you alert. Exercise improves blood flow to the brain and keeps you sharp and active to handle any challenging task.

- Exercise helps you work more. Exercise improves your overall health and provides you stamina to work more.

- Exercise improves your mental health: Exercise relieves stress and depression and improves your mental health. Exercise boosts serotonin production, which improves your mood and makes you feel better. When you are in a good mood, you will finish even complex task faster.

Think activity, not exercise. Make exercise a part of your life!

For most of us, exercise isn't a fun thing to do. It involves stretching, straining, and sweating, and after a hard day's work, no one is looking forward to it. So make exercise a part of your life:

- Don't use the car, walk your kids to school and jog home

- Walk faster when mowing the lawn

- Get off the train or bus one stop early and walk

- Do some stretching, jumping jacks or sit-ups while watching TV

- Whenever you get a chance, swim or walk

- Do some gardening every day

- Do things that you like, such as horseback-riding, bicycling, dancing and rope-jumping

Play a sport: baseball, basketball, golf, bowling or tennis.

Chapter 2: Organize Your Home, Office, Personal Life and Finance

Organize your home

Organizing your entire home will take a lot of time. So be productive and spend two hours every weekend to organize a small part of your house, such as closets, under the bed, and the walls of the garage.

- *Bedroom*: Don't keep anything under the bed, but if you have to, use boxes or plastic containers to place them. Use a basket for dirty clothes, and place all your used cloths in them.

- *Dining room and living room*: Spend 10 minutes every day cleaning clutter from the coffee table, dining table, couch and living room floor. Buy a small basket or bins for every member of your family and put all the appropriate items in individual bins.

- *Kitchen*: Remove all duplicate dishes, pots and utensils from your kitchen. Arrange the plastic ware in a matching order, and build shelves or cabinets in your pantry for canned items. Make a list before going to the grocery store and buy only from the list. Use see through plastic boxes in the refrigerator.

o *Bathroom*: Place small baskets or use dividers in the drawer. Put individual toothbrushes, body care and cosmetics on separate bins.

o *Attics and basements*: Don't leave items on the floor. Build shelves on the walls and use plastic boxes. Place a labeled plastic container for every member of the family in the attic or basement. Put frequently used items in the front and rarely used items in the back.

o *Garage*: Install shelves in the walls. Use clear plastic container to store items, and install hooks on the walls and ceiling pegs to place bikes, tools and sports equipment.

o Don't keep items just because they have sentimental value. Store all the unused items in a box for a month and donate or sell them after a certain time.

o *Digitize everything:* Digitize your old DVD's and CD's, photos and remove the excess.

Organize your office for an organized work day

Clutter in the office or workplace creates an uninviting work environment, makes you disorganized, lowers efficiency and productivity. Follow these tips to clutter free your work place:

o *Organize your work area:* Organize your work area and place office equipment, such as closet, filing cabinets, drawers, shelves and other work related items, in appropriate places.

o *Organize your desk:* Label all of your bins and filing systems. This will ensure easy access to documents and a smooth work process. Arrange your filing systems and work according to significance, and finish them one by one. Use a file drawer for the follow-up filing system and label the folders in arranging to work order like today, tomorrow, next week, and next month.

o *Filing cabinets*: Label your file-folders and arrange them in appropriate categories. Use an external hard drive and scanner to avoid paper use, and once a year, clear out all your filing cabinets.

o *Organize your computer*: Appropriately label all files on your work computer and make it easy to navigate. Make sure others can find relevant files without your help, and delete unused and old archive files.

o *Change your environment*: Working long periods of time indoors in artificial light causes "nature deficit disorder" and reduces productivity. Make your office space environment friendly, so bring nature inside with plants and natural green photography. Work in an open space now and then.

Develop habits for an organized life:

- o *Write down everything*: Write down all of your important events and activities. Your laptop and smartphone will make writing really easy for you. Write down everything, such as important appointments and meetings, birthdays, grocery shopping list, doctor's appointment and holiday gifts.

- o *Create schedules and maintain deadlines*: Create realistic schedules and deadlines and maintain them for a productive day. Make a bucket list.

- o *Maintain a routine*: Follow a routine for cleaning things from your house and office, such as digital cleanup routine, house cleaning routine and laundry routine. Fix a weekly timetable for cleanup.

- o *Emergency file system*: Build an emergency file system for important documents, such as financial statements, tax documents, mortgage or lease papers, insurance documents, medical records and passports.

o *Manage your Internet life and remain productive*: Distractions are part of daily life and nobody can avoid it entirely. For an organized, productive life, you need to limit distractions. In this day and age, the Internet and social networks have become the biggest distraction for everyone. Set a certain time of the day to check your Facebook, Twitter, emails and other social media accounts, and avoid checking them every few minutes. Smartphones are another distraction. Some calls are very important, but if you are always busy answering phone calls, it will be hard for you to stay focused on the job at hand. When you are busy with your work, turn the phone off and schedule the business calls just like in-person business meetings.

Manage your finances for an organized life

o *Limit unnecessary spending*: Impulsive spending has become a big burden for many of us. Before going to the superstore and market, make a detailed list and buy only from the list. Start to make the list a few days early to include everything you need. Avoid Wal-Mart and shopping malls when you want to go outside and relax, go to the park or walk on the beach instead.

o *Evaluate expenses*: Keep a detailed list of all your expenses for one month, don't leave out any expenses. Decide which items you don't need, and for the next months, buy only the necessary items and avoid the unnecessary stuff.

o *Invest*: Prepare early in life and make a sound investment to keep your family secure. Start a retirement plan early in your life. Starting early will help you to save the maximum amount for your family. You can take a life insurance and try other insurances, such as homeowners or leaseholder's insurance.

o *Avoid debts*: Avoiding debts are a really good idea. But life is not easy, so if you have a student loan or personal loans, credit cards or any other debt, start a debt elimination plan. Start to pay off your debt on a weekly basis, even it is a small amount, like $50 or $100. This could take a few years to pay off your loan, but it's essential and rewarding for you.

o *Automate bill payments*: Set up a automated bill payment system for your utility, credit card and other bills

Chapter 3: Manage Stress and Become More Productive and Organized

Stress drains your hope and energy, suffocates you mentally and lowers your organizational skills. Stress is the main cause of mental illness and makes you depended on others, and if you are mentally dependent on others, you can't be organized and productive in life.

Manage stress

Nowadays, life is complex, stressful and sometimes it becomes too much to handle. Gradually, you become unorganized, unproductive and dependent on others. Stress management start with identifying the root cause of stress in your life. Many of us manage stress in unhealthy ways, like drinking or smoking, using recreational drugs, under eating or overeating. However, you have to manage stress in a positive, healthy way and remain productive.

Productive ways to manage stress:

- *Avoid unnecessary stress*: Understand your capacity to deal with stressful events, and learn to say no in your professional and personal life. Limit exposure to the people who stress you out, and avoid topics that make you stressful.

- *Learn from the past*: When it's not possible to avoid stressful situations, then remember past experiences and cope with the current situation. If it is necessary to compromise, for instance, you want someone to change his or her behavior towards you, change your behavior first and set an example for him or her to follow.

o *Start a stress journal*: Start a stress journal. It will help you to identify your stress triggers, and you will be able to deal with them with relative ease. In your stress journal, write down the events that causes you stress, how you feel emotionally and physically, what is your response to stress and what you do to make things better.

o *Do things that you enjoy:*

- Spend time in nature and regularly walk in the park

- Call your friends and have conversations

- When you are feeling stressed, do some exercise

- Take a bubble bath and light scented candles

- Enjoy a warm cup of coffee or tea

- Get a relaxing massage

- Read a book, listen to music or watch a comedy

Whenever you are facing a stressful situation, think the positives in your life and good things that happened and will continue to happen in the future.

Main benefits of meditation in your life:

o Meditation rejuvenates your mind and body

o Meditation boosts your memory and improves your focus on work

o Mediation keeps you active and organized throughout the day

o Meditation increases blood flow to the brain cells and make them more active

o Meditation manages your stress and doesn't cost you anything

Mindfulness meditation to relieve stress

Mindfulness teaches you keeping your attention in the present moment, without judging it good or bad, happy or sad. Mindfulness shows you to live each moment as mindfully and as fully as possible. Mindfulness is not just a relaxation technique - it's an attitude toward productive living.

To start practicing mindfulness, sit comfortably on a chair or on the floor and keep your head, neck and back straight, but don't make them stiff. Then:

o Concentrate on a simple object, ideally on your breathing. Pay attention on the feeling of the air as it goes in and out of your body with each breath. Don't try to control the breathing by slowing it down or speeding it up, just observe the breathing.

o Even when you are completely focused on the breathing, your mind will wander off. Notice where your mind went, perhaps to a distant memory or an upcoming event, and then gently return your focus to your breathing.

o Use your breathing as an anchor. Each time your mind wanders off, observe where it went, momentarily acknowledge it and gently return your attention to breathing.

o Let go all your thoughts and worries, just keep breathing and keep your mind on the present moment.

o Practice for five minutes and then gradually increase the time to 10, 20 or to 30 minutes.

Mindfulness is very easy to practice, and you can apply it to anything, such as showering, eating, working, running errands, talking or when playing with your kids.

Chapter 4: Avoid Multitasking and Follow Productive Methods for an Organized Life

Multitasking and productive life

Multitasking simply means doing two or more tasks at the same time or quickly switching from one task to another. It's a concept of doing a few tasks at once, like making a call, composing an email, posting a tweet, checking messages and doing office work. Scientists have found that only 2% of the entire population is born with multitasking ability and the other 98% are unable to perform multitasking successfully and have damaging side effects.

Multitasking reduces productivity

Multitasking is controlled by your brain's mental executive functions, and this executive function manages cognitive processes of the brain and takes decision to when, how and in which order tasks should be done. The cognitive functions work in two stages: choosing which task to do first and switching from one task to another.

You now have a good idea about how the human brain works. It is designed to focus on one job at a time, and once it's finished, move on to another. However, when you are multitasking and switching from one task to another within a few seconds, you are permanently damaging your brain. Separate research conducted by Stanford University and University of Sussex found that individuals who multitask can't remember information correctly and are unable to focus to complete a task successfully. According to the Journal of Experimental Psychology, multitasking lowers productivity by 40%.

Here are a few examples of how multitasking lowers your productivity:

o If you concentrate on one task, you will finish it faster and switching between tasks will take more time to finish all the tasks successfully.

o Task switches force you to make more errors.

o Errors will increase dramatically if you are doing a few complex tasks at once.

o Task switches add up and you become less productive.

Solve the multitasking problem

o *Only do one task:* If you are trying to write, then don't watch the TV, or if you are reading or organizing office work, then don't concentrate on your Facebook account.

- *Exception for some:* One study shows that some people can concentrate on a mental task while they are busy with another physical task, but this is not for everyone.

- *The 80/20 rule*: It's also known as "Pareto Principle." It means that 80% of the effects come from 20% of the causes. Identify the 20% of the tasks you are really good at and finish them one after another.

- *Start with the important task first*: Start the most important task first, as this will make you relaxed and avoid anxiety to jump into multitasking.

Productivity methods for a productive life

If you want an organized life, applying a proven productivity method is the right step towards it. These methods will help you waste less time on thinking and spend your valuable time on doing things.

- *The Pomodoro Method*: In the early 1990's, Francesco Cirillo created the Pomodoro technique. You only need a timer and self-discipline to start this method. Set a timer for 25 minutes, start the timer, and then start working. Continue to work for 25 minutes and when the alarm goes off; take a break for 5 minutes. This is called one "pomodoro". Repeat this process of working and take a longer break (15-20 minute) after 4 pomodoros. Working and taking breaks help you to stay focused on the job and feel rested.

o *GTD or Getting things done:* David Allen invented the GTD or getting things done productivity method as detailed in his famous book *Getting Things Done.* GTD shows you quickly can organize and easily implement your ideas. GTD also encourages people to organize to-do-lists according to priority. The things that are important should be done first. Large tasks should be broken into small manageable pieces to finish easily and quickly. This method is so popular with ordinary people that there are classes, blogs, seminars and apps available to help people to apply in their lives.

o *Don't Break the Chain*: "Don't Break the Chain" was invented by Jerry Seinfeld. It's a simple productivity method and encourages individuals to keep working on important matters and successfully reach their goals. Following this method is easy: start any task that you want to do, finish it and then repeat the process to make it a habit. After finishing every task, mark it down on a calendar. Over time these marks will encourage you to keep doing the tasks that you want and "don't break the chain."

- *Franklin Planner*: Franklin Covey invented this method in 1984. This planner is just like a personal organizer. It consolidates appointments, tasks and personal notes in one place. This planner helps users to organize their whole week, not just a single day.

- *The Action Method*: Behance Software Company invented this action method. Users are really fond of this software because it emphasizes achieving goals and finishing work.

- *Custom personal method*: Sometimes people combine several useful elements of multiple productivity methods and create their own personal method to organize their life. A popular combination of GTD and Pomodoro. Think about the elements that best suit you and combine them.

Chapter 5: Useful Tips for a Productive life

Helpful tips for a productive life:

- *Plan your day early:* Fix 15 minutes of every evening to plan out the next day. With a plan, you can jump-start the next day. You will have a clearly defined purpose, and you can focus on each task and move on to another task when it's finished. Here, there is no possibility of wasting time when you have a plan.

- *Take advantage of morning and evening commute*: Take advantage of morning and evening commutes by taking notes with your phone or listening to some relaxing music or audio book.

- *Before any meeting*: Take advantage of time before a meeting, for example, if you are waiting for someone to show up or arrived early at a meeting, use this time to finish some small tasks. Check your to-do-list, draft an important email you need to write, read an important document again, etc.

- *Elevator*: When you are in the elevator, check your messages and emails, or add some tasks to your to-do-list.

○ *Schedule your personal time:* Continuously working makes you stressed and leads to fatigue. Schedule some personal time and maintain it. Spend time with family members, close friends or develop a hobby.

Apps to organize your day:

○ *Google calendar*: You probably know about this wonderful tool from Google. Google calendar is an excellent app to help you keep track of your appointments and daily tasks. You can create events, make recurring events and invite others.

○ *Astrid:* You can create a to-do-list from your laptop and smartphone with Astrid's help. This app will allow you to integrate Google calendar and emails.

○ *Dropbox*: Dropbox is a well-known and trusted backup service. You can synchronize and backup your important documents, notes and projects. You can use your iPad, laptop or smartphone to use Dropbox.

○ *Evernote:* Evernote is another organizational tool to help you gather and organize everything you need.

o *Instapaper:* Instapaper is really useful when you want to save time. You can save blog posts and articles to a reading list with it and read them later from your smartphone, laptop or Kindle.

Conclusion

As you can see, you just have to follow some simple steps to enjoy productive and stress free organized life. It's time to stop wasting time and move your life forward in an organized way. Hope this book helped you in your quest.

Good luck.

Made in the USA
Lexington, KY
26 March 2017